Lessons from the Heart:
Navigating Life

Hyacinth C. Foster

authorHOUSE®

AuthorHouse™
1663 Liberty Drive
Bloomington, IN 47403
www.authorhouse.com
Phone: 1-800-839-8640

First published by AuthorHouse 7/22/2011

ISBN: 978-1-4567-5324-5 (e)
ISBN: 978-1-4567-5325-2 (sc)

Library of Congress Control Number: 2011908040

Printed in the United States of America

Any people depicted in stock imagery provided by Thinkstock are models,
and such images are being used for illustrative purposes only.
Certain stock imagery © Thinkstock.

This book is printed on acid-free paper.

Hyacinths, hyacinths...the true beauty of nature. In shades of cream, yellow, peach, pink, salmon, orange, lavender, blue, and purple. They will satisfy your sense of sight and smell everyday of each year. Plant them in the fall they will arrive in the spring. Your happiness is ensured from one season to the next!

My name—**Hyacinth**—has been the source of my inspiration since I learned to spell the name at age eleven. I was forced to do so when I had to complete the Common Entrance examination in Jamaica, an island in the Northern Caribbean and to the southwest of Florida. Before that time, I was Carmen, and still am to my immediate family. Recently, my son confessed how embarrassed he was that he could not spell his mother's name as a child. I have learned to deal with mispronunciations, misspellings, and misconceptions of whether I am a male or a female, but nonetheless, the name has always been my source of laughter, amazement, and joy in the many changes of my life.

And, changes there have been! Each change came after major upheaval in my life. However, I want everyone to know my belief that each person has a destiny, and you cannot change that. You can fight it or you can just take it where it leads you. This book will help you to understand that wherever you find yourself, at any given moment in time that is where you are supposed to be. There are lessons to be learned as you meet those upheavals. This book illustrates the lessons, and I want to have them in writing to help my children, Trudy and Gregg; the individuals that I call friends, and all others who read this book. Remember, you are a product of all the people with whom you interact each day of life. There are lessons in those interactions be they good or negative.

In these episodes, you will not learn about the great upheavals that were negative. I discovered that if I focused on the negatives then I shut down my happiness potential, and may forget about what is important in life—caring about others! I prefer to learn from them and use them as the stepping stones in my 20 most important **life lessons**. You will recognize that sub-lessons are sometimes necessary, but I chose the number 20 to remember the day we laid Mom to rest—May 20, 1989.

As you travel with me through the mazes of the lessons, you will recognize that some lessons came at the end of one session! Other lessons developed through the intertwining of the stages of the journey called LIFE.

A good score on the Common Entrance Examination, at age eleven, ensured a scholarship to enter boarding school. I would score big time! This would be the greatest training of my life. A new life awaited me! I would no longer be the lone child in a household, but I would get to make new friends and live at boarding school, with other teenagers from all over the island of Jamaica. By the way, sometimes, there would be students from other far away countries including other Caribbean islands and Europe! The greatest adjustment came from not feeling one was poor compared to others. You see, everyone came to boarding school with the same type and amount of clothing, same type of shoes, same type of sheets, and even the same type of socks. The list of required apparel, food, and books was checked carefully, by the administration, at the beginning of each school term. Parents were notified immediately of any missing items and they had to be mailed in within the first week of the term. The only way of differentiating each student's possessions was that each item had to be clearly labeled with individual's initials.

Now, back to the controversy surrounding my name! At the beginning of this phase, I discovered the correct order of my names and the correct spellings. Up until this age, I was known as Carmen... Do not ask for Hyacinth, it will take a while before any family member realizes to whom you are referring.

TABLE OF CONTENTS

LIFE LESSON #1:

Think carefully about naming your child.
He or she will have that name for a long time!

Knowledge of my name came about in quite an unusual manner. Many children in Jamaica are called by some other name than the one that appears on their birth certificates, and in addition, you will find many girls with name of flowers! -- Rose, Heather, Lilly, Pansy, and Violet— Mine was no exception—**HYACINTH**. I never knew this flower, in real life, until I came to the United States in 1985. Before, I could only relate to the name through photographs. You have seen these flowers in full bloom during the early spring. The flowers have a powerful and strong, but awesome odor. The tiny flowerets come in shades of purple/ lavender (my favorite), yellow, pink, red, blue white, salmon, and orange.

Well, I learned my new name and how to spell it in less than 10 minutes. I was seated in the Common Entrance Examination room at the local primary school, in Alderton District, Jamaica. The examination that would determined my life as a possible student of the academics, was about to begin. This was my first major examination. My sense of fear was overwhelming, my heart was racing, and my palms were sweating. I was in another world, but I was brought back to reality quickly when I became aware of the attendance calling—M. C, P. D, R. S, F. R—sounding breathless Miss R, the elderly spinster was now in fast motion—J. W, N. W, and finally E. W. You could hear Miss R's heavy breathing as she approached what could have been the fortieth name, and as she continued her movement around the room.

So what was happening? I did not hear my name! Well, let me wait! Maybe she had skipped over **J—Johnson** (my maiden name) in her haste to get us started on the exam. Without any notice, her voice boomed, "Which child has not heard his or her name?" Slowly my hand rose. I was so scared because Miss R looked like a giant to a tiny child like me. "What is your name?" I said softly, "Carmen Johnson". "I did not hear you, she said!" I tried a little louder! My mouth was suddenly dry! Where was the saliva? I could see and feel her impatience with me. What was happening? I was always good with my mouth! Talk never failed me before! I found my voice and answered a little louder, **Carmen Johnson**. This was a battle waiting to happen, and so I shut my mouth quickly after I gave the answer for the second time. This was not the way to begin an exam!

I was a bit taken back by my own bashful behavior. I was a child that could not be easily intimidated. I think I had found my match today! No one in the large room made a sound, and each of my friends sat as if on military duty. We were all at assigned desks that were in perfect rows with what appeared to be identical spacing.

Well, now Miss R displaying total disgust with the situation or with me, blared, "You are not only **Carmen Johnson**, you are **Hyacinth Carmen Johnson—LEARN IT NOW**!" This was going to be a monumental task. I could not pronounce the name let alone spell the name! Well, intervention came from where I do not know because she wrote the long name—**EIGHT letters**—with heavy black ink on a piece of white paper—**HYACINTH**—there was no rhyme or reason to the letters. It was the longest word I had ever seen. Much longer that any of the words I had learned for the Intelligence test which would begin any minute and would start with the *Analogies —socks is to foot as hat is to head, leaf is to tree as petal is to flower.* "One minute to go", Ms. R said—"Take up your pencils now, and turn to page one, the Analogies section".

At that moment, I still had to learn the spelling of my new name that needed to be written at the top of each page and at the same time focus on the test questions. Surely, I would fail! Let me explain, those examinations came straight from Great Britain to be administered to the young colonists of the Caribbean islands. The scores on the examinations would determine the next phase of learning for each child in the room. Some of us would go on an academic journey, others would travel the technical route, while who knows what would be the fate of many others.

The examination consisted of various sections— English—the sections on grammar and composition, to be followed by—Math and Science—that were compulsory. What was evaporation again? Should I move the decimal point to the right or left when dividing or was it when multiplying? How many furlongs were in a mile? Were there

14 or 15 pounds in a stone? Was Cuba 90 or 95 miles due North of Jamaica?

Panic, fear, and anxiety were around me. Not to mention the need to use the bathroom after the stressful experience, but that was out of the question! There was only one break after the first section–one hour away—I could see this ticket slipping away and all because of that name—**HYACINTH**! Ever so often, one of my friends would glance at me with pitiful eyes, and Ms. R became my close companion. She moved around my space as if she was the sergeant who expected me to disappear into the floor. I would not be intimidated! I heard my father saying—"You must take charge"—I listened!— That name—**HYACINTH**—was the source of my problem during that examination, and I made a pact with myself that if I ever had children, they would have no more than five letters in their first names. They would be able to spell that name early, VERY early in life. No one would ever call them by another name other than their given names. And now, you understand why my daughter's name is **TRUDY** and my son is **GREGG.**

Trudy

Gregg

The school system, in Jamaica, is different from that of the United States. It is a prototype of the Colonial rule, the British, and its educational system. Children start school at age seven in "A" class. By the time I began, the work was so easy, considering that I was so well prepared by my father that boredom began to set in. Luckily, the teacher, Miss B., recognized the situation and so I was placed in the "B" class. Still, I advanced to the forefront of that new class, but I remained there with eight-year-old children and to spare me further boredom, I was given extra class work.

In the educational system, if children proved themselves capable of advanced work, their age became irrelevant. In time, I was always in a class with older children. I guess you can imagine what that did to me. That peculiarity of associating with older students would serve me well when I entered boarding school and found that the young women in my class were one year my senior. I felt right at home with this situation!

Well, the results of the Common Entrance Examination came six months later, and I was awarded a full scholarship to high school. My living, tuition, books, and all fees—**well everything** would be paid for by the government. I was on my way to becoming a scholar at age 11. I waited anxiously for September 1st to arrive, but as the day grew closer, I became more apprehensive. The day did arrive and I was packed with all my belonging in three large suitcases, plus my *tuck-box*. The *tuck-box* was a wooden cube, built by my father, and contained crackers, sweetie (candies), cream soda, jam, jellies, cookies, knives, forks and spoons plus other foods that would help to placate my transition to this new environment. I was ready for the new adventure, but I felt a mixture of emotions. Anxiety and excitement we closely interwoven in this situation!

Survival without my father was a foreboding thought. Deep down I knew that somehow he would find a way to reduce any fears. Well, every Saturday throughout the school year, he came to visit. He always had a small case of snacks and my pocket money. My mother made sure to express her displeasure with the way I was being spoilt by my father. He never made any comment and he just kept on doing whatever he could for me. As I reflect on his actions, I now understand why I have succeeded in spoiling my own children.

I struggle to find words to describe the adjustment to this new life at boarding school. My life at Ferncourt High School was controlled by a bell! That bell would ring: to wake you up; to begin and end your shower; to start eating; to stop eating; to clear the dining table; to go to class; at the end of each class period; to go to lunch; to end lunch; to go to prep (homework) time; to go to supper; to begin and end activity (needlework) or reading time; to get ready for bed; lights out.

The next day, the process of bell ringing would be repeated and for the following five days—Mondays through

Fridays with only small variations on Saturdays and Sundays. You get the idea! Later, I would learn that ringing a bell helps to clear negativity from the environment. Also, my years of learning science has taught me that ringing of a bell is used to condition animals. So, I guess I was conditioned in a positive way!

Saturdays, at boarding school was special. It was the day to collect laundry that was done during the week by the laundry services. We could also visit the town to purchase any special items at the few stores on Main Street, Claremont, St. Ann, Jamaica. The day would include completing homework for the next week. In the late afternoon, we would get to watch a movie, *My Fair Lady*, became a staple. I still know the words to every song in that movie. At other times, we went to the "fete" where we danced until 10:30 p.m. This time was considered late by all accounts and we were always under the watchful eyes of the teachers and prefects.

Sundays was the day of rest at boarding school. Every girl went to church clothed in white: dress, shoes, socks, and hat. You had to be near death to be excused from this mission! We were told that it was important to use those visits to build our character, and develop discipline as young women. By the way, all clothes had to match perfectly. All shoes had to be polished and shined on Saturday. Even at this stage of my life, I continue to polish and shine my shoes! We walked in pairs to church which lasted for two long hours and we were under constant surveillance, to sit up straight and participate—sing even if you could not carry a tune! Failure to do so would involve loss of some privilege or the other once we returned to school.

LIFE LESSON #2:

Be comfortable in your own home.
Love your company.

Before my entry to boarding school life, school for me was sheer joy. Well, there was no other outlet except church! In addition, television did not arrive in my district until 1962. Therefore, entertainment was my design with the assistance of one of my sisters. Our games were original and were created as the need arose. The one radio was my father's monopoly for exclusive use by him in order to hear the evening news or connect with information from Cuba or Bonaire. It would be later that I would come to recognize my desire to visit both of these islands.

After seven o'clock in the evening, all listening to information from Jamaica ceased since the frequency in our remote area of the island was totally wiped out by the strong Cuban radio frequency. As if on cue, my father would launch into stories about his life while he lived in Cuba. At other times, we would get a clear picture of the grandparents who were dead long before I was born.

I was the leader even though I was the youngest child. I was just a plain mischievous, curious, and creative child! One episode has stayed with me! It is *Harvest* service at church. Let me give you the background—during this service all children bring some food kind that they actually tended over the year as an offering. The altar would be loaded with all manner of *fruits*—mangoes, oranges, star apple, guinep, and grapefruits: *food kind*—yam, potatoes (red and white), sugar cane, cocoa; *animal products* including eggs, meat, and fish. Not to be outdone by cakes and all manner of Jamaican dishes. Those would be sold off in a large outdoor market at the end of the service. Eggs were the main gifts of boys and girls who had raised a chicken and collected their own eggs for offering. All children were dressed in the latest fashions, and filed into church, two at a time, to the song –*Come, Ye Thankful People Come, Raise the song of harvest home.*[1]

The outfits for that particular year came from my aunt in New York, and included special fancy shoes to match my red and grey dress—gray top with a broad red color and pleated red and gray skirt. So, who ever heard of children wearing colored shoes when the latest children styles were white or black patent shoes? These shoes came with straps that could be worn in a *Mary-Jane* fashion at the front or at the back of the shoes. Now you know why I have always

---

1   My Methodist Hymn Book

worn *Mary Jane* dress shoes! Well, the shoes that I had to wear were not only the exact matching color of my dress, but they had **platform soles**!

I decided then and there that I would not be seen dead or alive in my shoes. I left home wearing the shoes that twisted sideways as I walked because I had never worn those types of shoes before. Oh! By the way, to get the perfect measure for the shoes, Mom traced my feet on paper that was then dispatched to my aunt so I would receive my gift by October and harvest time.

Just before we lined up to march to the altar, in pairs, I hid the shoes and walked with head held high in my white socks up to the altar! Surely, no one would notice! That did not happen! Miss O, the children's organist, saw and immediately informed my mother. As I sat down to enjoy the service, I was gently lifted out of the bench, and with my Mom crying from embarrassment, I had to sit out the service in the vestry. I did not care though. I would take my punishment when I got home. Why should I cry before then! Don't they think that I was embarrassed also—those shoes! You can imagine what happened when I got home from church! My escapades continued unabated but my father thought that I was such a dear little girl so I missed a great deal of punishment!

Occasionally, I was allowed to visit my favorite aunt, Auntie Fay, on a Saturday night. That was the total of my socialization, except for Church, and Sunday school. As a result, books became my closest friends. There were very few children books about Jamaican life, so all my experiences came from books that were written by British authors. I knew most of the nursery rhymes that were ever written and every edition of the Winnie-the-Pooh books. While reading those stories my imagination grew and I became lost in another life and time. England and the English countryside became my home! My voracious reading habit and expanding vocabulary continue to present day.

There was another great teacher in my life—my father— the preacher, banker, teacher, and village consultant on all matters! I followed him everywhere and he taught me about everything that mattered in life. I learned to listen attentively to others and show care and concern. I learned to do the chores that were considered boy-stuff. I could eventually paint an entire house; cut the limbs from a small tree; do gardening (a past time in which I continue to engage); climb any tree; and even ride a donkey. I became an expert at using a hammer and nails; a plane and level as an accomplished builder. In addition, my father taught me to do the books which were a part of his job as manager of the small bank (the village Credit Union).

This was my training and lessons in honesty and integrity. As I grew up, I became disenfranchised with the way some fathers disappear from their children's lives. I believe that the absences have lasting effects on the children in our society. **This is for the men**—Do not have children if you will not be there! I have witnessed the consequences of your absences on so many children during my career as an educator. Help your children while you are able. You will not be here forever!

On Friday, August 1, 1968 at 1:00 pm, my father looked at me then he looked in the same direction where his eyes were focused when he had last spoken. He pointed his fingers in the directions, squeezed my hand, took two deep breaths and he was gone forever. Suddenly, everything became deathly quiet. My mother was crying quietly, but then she began to scream. Someone went to call the undertaker and everyone tried to calm down my mother.

This was a small village and news of the death traveled quickly, more like a fire. I had never lost anyone who was so close to me. It is a very strange feeling, as if one is in a dream and would wake up to find that nothing that happened was true. Once my father's body was taken away, any entire host of people, many of whom I did not know came and never left. This was all so strange! People volunteered to cook meals on a non-stop basis, and everyone ate. There seemed to be no end to the cooking eating and singing, this was round the clock process, morning, noon, and night for eight days and nights.

There was no privacy to be found in my once private home. My father had insisted on ultimate privacy for his family when he was alive. People could only come to the drawing room; no one could come into the bedrooms. I guess

I now know why I do not like to have people in my bedroom! Well, this invasion continued unabated each day. I wondered when it would stop. Well, nothing would stop, I was told, until after my father's funeral. Here was my induction into a "nine-night." This was a Jamaican tradition which is more like an extended wake. I tried to imagine how we would survive. Well, if the day were crowded, the nights were much worse. People set up an area for singing. The songs were so mournful and were sung without much unison and as loud as possible. The "festivities" included a self-appointed leader who knew all the words of each song by heart. He or she called out the lines and the gathering repeated those words. There were no musical instruments involved, only voices. A deputy would take over and continue the process when the leader was tired. That ceremony continued all night until the sun came up. Next night, the process of singing and eating continued… for nine nights…without fail. I really did not know how much more one could deal with! Then people kept expressing how sorry they were feeling for us. I wondered why they felt this way.

After all, at this time, I was the last child and my father has provided for us, taught us all very well and had imprinted in each of us the need to get adequate education. He had made me promise to continue my education and I do not make light of promises. I think this was the time when I learned that if you are asked to do anything and you find it impossible, you need to say **NO**. I have now perfected the art of saying, **NO**. If I say I will do anything, I will do it no matter what. This lesson would come to serve me well, later in life. I have often explained to Trudy and Gregg the importance of not saying Yes when you actually mean No. In this way, you maintain your integrity.

My father's funeral was on August 10, 1968. The entire village was at a standstill and the service was long. Once again, people continued to express fear as to how we would cope. I would have preferred that they said nothing. Maybe then, the pain would go away faster. This was the time when I made a pledge that would try to be there for friends or families who lost loved ones and I would try to be there with a quiet strength. Sometimes the less said the better. After the funeral, I stayed home with my mother and got the house back into a semblance of order before returning to school.

My boarding school life was approaching an end. I worked hard at school but I also had fun. I also learned to deal with my father's death. I visited my mother very often and she traveled more often to visit her children in Kingston, the capital city of Jamaica. My mother seemed to be dealing well with the loss in her life but I could also see that she was lonely. She never discussed her feelings with me until I was much older. It was also at this time that I realized how much my father respected my opinions and me. He made me the executor to his last will and testament

One of the many lessons in my life came from my weekly Sunday experiences at boarding school. After church and lunch, there was a period of rest! One could only read in the silence. Reading continues to be one of my favorite hobbies. The silence did become part of my internal clock! Eventually, I grew real tired of the silence. I would always try to have some background voices wherever I was seated. However, in retrospect, all of the silence has helped me to love myself and be able to stay by myself for endless hours. I am my best friend! ***Practice loving your own company.*** The lessons gained in boarding school and the structure developed were many and they continue to be oh, so relevant today! My gratitude will always be to my headmaster, Mr. F. He has molded so many lives including mine!

LIFE LESSON # 3:

A place for everything, and everything in its place.

Boarding school continued to be the greatest force in my life. The boarding schools in Jamaica were designed for boys and girls, ages eleven through seventeen—grades 7 through 11. However, the dorms were either males or females. Although males were separated from the females for living arrangements, both sexes attended classes together and participated in all social activities. During that time, some of my best friends were males. That feature continued into my adult life.

Boarding school life was a time of learning and changes. Remember, I had to learn this new name—**HYACINTH**—and adjust to being called by this name; no longer did anyone mention the name, Carmen. I only wrote the name Carmen when completing examination papers or other official documents. With the name **HYACINTH**, I found that I was living in two worlds. When I went home for school vacations, I became **Carmen** or **Carms.** Then, when I returned to school, I would once again be—**HYACINTH**. I survived in those two worlds for five years, and thought that would be the end, but living in these two worlds has continued until today. Does it have a psychological effect on me? Maybe, but I have developed coping skills, I guess! **Remember think carefully about naming your children**!

If I believed the adjustment with my name was the only issue, I was mistaken. Boarding school was a whole new world! I had to learn to sleep in a large room, filled with forty, double bunk beds. If you arrived late at the beginning of the term, you had to take the top bunk. There were no steps to climb up to the top bunk; you jumped! In this dorm, there was a space to hang your clothes, a place to put your shoes, a place to put your books, a place to put your snacks. A place for every earthly possession! In fact, there was a place for everything! Nothing could be out of place; otherwise, you would be punished. This usually meant that you could not go with the others to the movies or the dance on Saturday. HOWEVER, you had to go to Church on Sunday!

I missed many of those social sessions as one can imagine. It took quite a few years for me to "get it". As a result, I did not get the dancing instruction that I desperately needed during those years. Remember who my father was? To this day, the true skill of dancing has passed me by. Dance classes will begin in earnest after this book is completed! More importantly, I became an extremely organized individual. My children had the hardest time dealing with me at home.

Everything has to be in its correct place and I maintain a very clean home—A good trait to pass on to your children.

The years at boarding school were the greatest periods of my formal and informal learning. I developed a love for all ideas connected with science. And, I became adept in money management; developed a plethora of negotiation techniques that ran the gamut from money transactions to academic grades; built up a good understanding of the term, friend; and became an independent spirit! In addition, I became the great risk-taker and I learned to express the word, *No,* with conviction coupled with gentleness. As my formal education continued, I never lived at home, except for holidays, after the age of eleven. I was forced to grow up and mature from all of these external experiences.

Many years later as a teacher, for 15 years, at a Friends' school, by the way, my children attended the school; I would develop the skills to enjoy my company. The process of reflection in silence, finding your inner **LIGHT** that are principles of the Quaker educational philosophy would serve me well though many days of living and doing everything for myself. This was when all of father's lessons took on relevance. I continue to enjoy my company. I do not ever feel alone when I am by myself. Remember, your personal happiness comes from enjoying your own company as you reflect on actions that you need to take to promote yourself- **Develop comfort within your home so that you will always be at peace with your environment.**

Support and provide structure for your children- Not advocating for all that occurred here, you will see! –

And Life Lesson # 5: Speak your mind, and speak it clearly without any tone of rudeness.

The life in boarding school was very structured, if not regimented! A bell signaled all activities! How I hated the bell! I still find that I come to order whenever I hear a bell! As mentioned before, in a typical day, there was a time to get up, to go for a shower, breakfast, classes, snack, lunch, tea—scones and lemonade—(British tradition), games, dinner, homework (two hours in total silence), and finally bedtime and lights-out! (Lateness at any activity, including waking up was not to be tolerated, one would be punished. There were no novelty or ingenuity about the consequences, they did not change, in each case one was deprived of something, and there was not much to do anyway). I invented ways to spice up life.

Was this the start of my life as a scientist? *Trouble-maker and Cheeky (later shortened to Cheeks)* were the new names and I was the lawyer for any injustice. I advocated about the inequities between the students and the prefects (seniors). I advocated about the food in the dining room. You name it and there was an argument to be put forth by me. I became an ever-present body in the headmaster's office. As a result, my father became a frequent visitor to the campus. However, in his eyes, I could do no wrong! I was never suspended from school because I always maintained very good grades in my classes. In addition, I could be very outspoken in my comments, but those were never used against me because my tone was pleasant and never a rude word left this mouth! I just said things that were considered not nice coming from a child! I became very popular, and this trait resulted in many of my classmates following along with me.

However, I did not consider many of them my friends since in the face of trouble they disappeared. This trait of standing up to all forms of injustice has continued today. I have become very wise in choosing my friends and not allowing others to choose me as their friend. This has not always worked. Once again, Remember, your true friends will not disappear in the face of adversity!

LIFE'S LESSONS # 6:

You can only tell yourself your secrets, if told to others, these secrets will be repeated.

I learned this lesson the hard way while still at boarding school. At boarding school, a group of girls took joy in reporting everything to the authority. As a result, I was always in trouble because I got tired of following the rules. My friends and I decided that enough was enough! We planned to get back at the four reporters. One night we stayed up late and made a mixture of hair oil, toothpaste, and body talc (PASTE) and glue. The next night we put our plan into action. As soon as the girls were asleep, were gently layered large amount of the paste next to each girl's pillow and went to sleep. In the morning, there was pandemonium when the four reporters woke. Two of the girls had to go to the sick bay to have portions of their hair removed because the mixture could not be removed by simply washing. That was just the start to what was to come!

The entire dorm of forty girls was under interrogation

and threats of being suspended. We could not go back to classes until the culprits were discovered! At first, everyone stuck to their story and declared that they did not know who was responsible. However, as the threat of reporting to parents was added, those whom I called my friends laid the blame at my feet! My father had to come in yet again! He never told me of his discussion with the principal, but I was not suspended. Instead, I was isolated for one week. I was not allowed to attend any social events, not even church! Remember, this had to be serious when one did not attend church. For those long days, I was the social outcast.

Those consequences did not matter to me except for having to write 500 lines in two days—"Your behavior was unbecoming of a lady. If repeated, you will face not only suspension, but expulsion"—that task had to be written in clear cursive, with ½ inch space between each word, and two lines between each of the sentences. That assignment took the greater part of two days. I survived by thinking that I was writing to someone else since the sentences did not have *I* but *You*. Ah, the mind of a child!

I did benefit from that harsh punishment though! Firstly, I developed excellent writing skills that I still have today. Secondly, I am very careful as to the people I call friends. Lastly, if I do not want anything repeated, I tell no-one! One song by the late Bob Marley- a Jamaican icon—deals with that very issue of the fact that only your friends know your secrets therefore they are the only ones who can repeat those secrets. My next life lesson does not reflect any of the harsh punishments that I continued to receive as the system tried to mold me into the best human being and young woman!

LIFE LESSON #7:

Do not leave home without doing it—
Make you bed, EVERYDAY!

Simple, you say! Well, there is your answer to organization which I began to learn at boarding school and continued to perfect at every stage of my journey through. I had internalized that lesson very fast as I adjusted to the new life at boarding school. As I mentioned before, each dorm consisted of twenty double-bunk beds— one bed on the top and one below. So, there were 40 girls to a room. By the way, if you had the lower bunk, you had to hope that the person above did not have a problem with their bladder! It was not until about three years into my life at boarding school that the administration decided to place a heavy plastic cover under each top mattress. You can imagine how many girls were recipients of a very unpleasant experience!

We went to the bathroom for our showers, in groups starting at 6:00am each morning and again at 6:00 pm each evening. Each morning, the bed had to be made in a very specific way. In those days, there were no fitted sheets, only flat sheets. Therefore, the sheet covering the mattress had to be done with the one-third corner on these double-bunk beds. There were no ladders to climb up to the top bunk; a leap of faith would take you to the top bunk. So, there were many accidents, as you might imagine.

Just before breakfast which was at 7:00 am, each dorm prefect came in to examine that sheets had the proper corners, blanket were folded to the end of the bed (Yes, blankets had to be on the bed even in these hot temperatures of Jamaica, part of the British boarding school etiquette!). If the prefect did not take to you or you did not follow the guidelines, then your bed would be in disarray on your return from breakfast! What did that mean? You had to redo the bed and make it to class by 7:55 am. Otherwise, you were late and had to serve detention from 3:30-4:30 p.m. It seems like it would never end, but they called it training to produce young women.

I found the best way to deal with this situation. I used safety pins to attach the corners of my sheet to the mattress, but I had to remember to remove them each morning. You can imagine what happened when I forget to do so one morning! I dare not explain the punishment because in these days those prefects would be charged with abuse of a minor. Needless to say, I was under daily surveillance for the remainder of the school term.

The lesson of making my bed before has stayed with me. I guess the saying—*Train up a child in the way he should go: and when he is old, he will not depart from it—Proverbs 22:6*—must be true! When my day is full of stress, I always find comfort in the vision that I will return to the comfort of a well-made bed. My children had to do it each day, with much resistance, but I observe them as they continue to mature that they still make the bed EVERYDAY. That is what I am told!

The transition to cleaning at home from cleaning at boarding school was not a difficult one. It seems I have always been cleaning and continue to use cleaning as a way to release any stress in my life. I hear that some people use food to deal with stress, I just clean. Before my adventures at boarding school, Saturdays were known as the cleaning days while my parents went to the market in the nearby town. My older sisters were left in charge. As the younger ones, we had to shoulder the burden of cleaning. You may guess why! Isn't that what older siblings do to younger ones? Nothing has changed. Most people I meet describe me as totally organized, and that is where organization begins. It is so amusing to me to visit people's homes and they are making every effort to clean-up at the same time that you are entering. My son often comments that my level of cleanliness is not in the normal realm of everyone!

Still, I set aside one day each week, Saturdays, to thoroughly clean my home. Do not ask me to go anywhere until my home is cleaned. In that way, you only need to do minor cleaning during the week. As life throws all the changes at you, you will have peace of mind to be in a clean and orderly place. This leads me to my next life lesson.

Lesson # 8:

You can do it!

Somehow, I always seem to find the energy to do what needs to be done. Whether it is CLEANING, cooking, or grading papers. I just do it. I do not like to think that duties are piling up around me. I was given a plaque that expound the virtues of the name Hyacinth— *one who does what needs to be done tomorrow today*! That's me! I find it uplifting and tell myself that with a little effort, there is nothing that I cannot do–not wanting to be a procrastinator, but I look at it as—*you can do it!*

Those words were from my father and became part of me and as I adopted those values, I became formidable. When I thought, I would fail Mr. L's mathematics class because he cared more about the way you made the letter *A* in Algebra rather than showing the correct procedure to solve the mathematical problems. I heard my father say, *"You can do it!"* When I had to sit for eight subjects at the General Certificate of Education at Ordinary (GCE

'O' level) and was convinced I would fail mathematics, I heard my father—***"You can do it!" Believe me; I know that there is nothing one cannot do! Just sit still and give the problem some thought. You will be surprised!***

Well, some reflection is needed here! Children who received the required scores on *Common Entrance Examination*, a young child first standardized examination, enter *First Form* (7th Grade in US), at age 11 and were ensured a "free" education for the next five years of high school.

Students who are not successful in this examination took the *Technical School* examinations and entered either the technical high schools or the Island's trade schools. On reflection, my parents must have been relieved to see me go away to boarding school because my mother always verbalized that I needed discipline. Her observations came about because I was the last child of several children to a father who was to later become a local a preacher in the Methodist church. My father usually explained away a great portion of my *bad* behavior as *she is a growing child*, or *look how tiny she is*, and sometimes *she is the baby*. Those phrases were irritants to mother, as she would explain amusingly in my later years.

During the first five years of my high school tenure, all lessons were geared towards completing the *Cambridge University's General Certificate in Education* at *Ordinary Level* by *Fourth Form (11th Grade in US)*. The number of subjects and a grade of *one*, *two*, or *three* ensured that a student continued on to *Grades 12* and *13*. It was at this point that students chose an area of specialization: languages, science, art, or business, in two, related subject areas. In addition, all students had to take the *Use of English, West Indian History,* and a mathematics course. My formal studies as a science major began as I pursued Chemistry and Biology at *Grade 12*. At the end of *Grade 13*, students once again sat for the higher-level Examination-the Cambridge *University's General Certificate in Education* at *Advanced Level.*

The success on the *Grade thirteen* standardized examination afforded me a full scholarship to University of the West Indies' Natural Science program. That university was the only institution of higher learning on the island and it served students from all other Caribbean islands. *Grade 13* results were equivalent to the first year of undergraduate studies at universities in the United States and as a result, the Bachelor degree at the University of the West Indies and European Universities is completed in three years. Once again, it is necessary to explain that the academic program of higher education is also "free", so the scholarship funds that I qualified for were for living accommodation, clothing, and incidentals.

"You can do it"— those were my father's final counsel before he left me forever. Those words continue to push me forward as I would later complete two Masters' degrees, and I am in the final stages of my work on a Doctorate in Education. I intended to go to the top! My children understand my motto—**You can only be free when you acquire as much education and knowledge as is possible!**

Life's Lesson # 9:

People will try to convince you that they know what is right for you! You are the only person who knows what is right for you.

The days of boarding school ended. My father was gone and several well-intentioned individuals told that the best thing to do was to find a job since Mom had never worked and was not able to help me financially. I decided that I was not going to stop learning. No, way! I had found so much joy with Mr. G's chemistry class where I finally learned to spell—**thermometer**—that I was not going to stop now! I had battled with Trevor R. and Winsome B to get to the top in Chemistry! I could not stop now. Learning was too much fun! I made my decision with the support of my sister and guide—Madge!

So having decided, my brother who knew the Headmaster of Excelsior High in Kingston, Jamaica helped me to enroll in that school. Excelsior High School would be my place for the next two years. This change necessitated living with older brother and his family. My brother did everything to make my life as happy as possible. However, one of my lessons from boarding school would be needed here. I will stick to the saying—**if you cannot say anything nice about a situation or person, say nothing**—Therefore, you will understand why I will not discuss those experiences. The greatest comfort that I received came from my older sister, Madge, who was living in England. She helped me to deal with changing situations. She has continued to be my rock and support through every situation whether good or bad.

Madge (My sister and friend for life)

I graduated from Grade 13 two years later and I was finding the pain of my father's absence easier to bear. That new environment was the medicine that I needed in order to deal with my father's death. It was during this time that I would make my closest and life-long friendship with Bev. G.

Bev (My closest friend)

My happiest days of high school were spent at Excelsior High. Our science labs were to the south of the campus. We were not allowed to leave campus during the day, but we did through the back gate. We broke the rules because we could-Why not? We were 6th Formers—the top of the lot. We went downtown to shop when we shouldn't. All we had to do was remove our tie and green belt and we became students from the nearby school who also had the same cream skirt and blouse. We found ways to escape from campus through the back gate since our science labs were steps away from the back gate. The science classes were the greatest experiences. We dissected frogs, and every animal imaginable as required by the Advanced Level syllabus. Chemistry was fun! Botany and Zoology were on the same level of enjoyment. We learned the scientific names of so many plants including agave plant that we found in the hills. I have a healthy respect for the Agavaceae *durangenis* plant after learning of its potential medical and esthetic value! Maybe, you will read more about this fascinating species. I do not know if this plant species has special meaning in my life, but in the center of the home garden here in Georgia is a large member of the Agave family—Agave americana. Maybe there is a meaning, maybe not! I will wait and see!

My mathematics teacher Mr. P. was a great instructor who never allowed us to know that many of us would just barely make it through the examinations. One fact that came home much later was the heritage of my teachers. Since Jamaica was a colony of England until 1962, the greater number of my teachers, at the primary, secondary, and undergraduate studies were of British origin-a fact I would not internalize until my arrival in the United States. It was at this point when I realized that my intonation and spelling would sometimes be in conflict with that of the people in the United States.

High School Graduation

During my career as children learned more about where Jamaica existed on the map, I taught them about my culture and life on the island. Many children made great attempts to speak like me; they took holidays to the island; wanted to learn how to cook the unique island dishes; and became more curious about the life in other places. Isn't that how we go about creating the global child? I still cannot understand why color matter in this great big country of ours. Remember people are People! Treat them well and with respect, then you will forget color!

Life Lesson # 10:

Some places and people will impact your life forever.
Use the places to help you return in your imagination
and center yourself, and remember those people always.

As I mentioned before, during my final years of high school, I would meet my life-long friend, Bev. We had many adventures together–to the social to dinners any trip that was possible we were there! I was a frequent visitor to her home where her mom, Ms. May was always cooking and feeding us. Bev has remained the closest friend that I have even to the time of writing this book. Others from my group included: B. B, E. H, R. T, C. B. come to mind often and I wonder where they are now? You all impacted my life!

My best and lasting memory of one place I visited at this age has helped me to relax whenever the need arises. I will take you on a tour of this magical place. You will have the opportunity to see Fern Gully, a three-mile stretch of road lined with many different species of ferns as the road twists and winds through what I was told was once a river bed. The Seville great house the former home of many slaves is on the way, and you may even want to frolic along the slopes of Dunn's River Falls, Jamaica's own Niagara Falls. However, I would encourage you to travel with me to a unique ecological wonder, scenes from which were used in one famous James Bond Movie. Many Jamaicans refer to them as the Runaway Caves and the town is known as Runaway Bay. As I was told during my visit with my Botany class while in high school, the lake got its name from the green algae that can be found all over the walls of the cave- *Green Grotto*...

Those caves date back to the time of the first Jamaicans, the *Arawak Indians* also known as *Tainos*. As one of my students informed me recently, the Tainos were the indigenous people of many Caribbean islands, including Jamaica.

Once inside, you will realize that there are many smaller caves into which you will not be allowed. However, the special feature of my visit was to the wide open area with stalactites and stalagmites in colors that seem to change as you go by. This is the perfect place to see an example of the Tyndall Effect where every dust particle seems to be magnified in the rays of light. I guess my science learning has to be connected to everything about me!

At the bottom in the deepest part of the intestines is the – Lake - known by many who venture into these parts as the Crystal Lakes. I will always have a mental picture of this body of water that appears to be so transparent. From my history learning during high school, I recognized that this was the pathway for many slaves who wanted to escape the painful and harsh treatment of slavery. While you are there in Jamaica, I encourage you to visit Port Royal, Faiths Pen (for true Jamaican cuisine), and the Blue Mountains.

There are other places to which I travel, mentally, when I need to reconnect my spirit—*Liberty Science Center, New Jersey, USA, Dolan DNA Lab, Long Island, USA, Circus-Circus Hotel , Las Vegas, USA, and The Lion King Musical* [T] *on Broadway, New York.*

It is important for each of us to lock those memories inside. They will be sources of solace in the years to come. However, one of my other favorite places and the root of all my learning was the campus of the University of the West Indies, Mona, Jamaica. A visit there will allow you to feel as if you are in your own world. My happy, carefree life continued after graduating from high school. I moved into the university dorm and I lived in Irvine Hall, a residence for males and females.

At Irvine Hall, there were blocks A-G with the female students in the front dorms and the males in the back. There was the Hall pledge which is not in any visible place, but has remained in my mind. The pledge asked that we students should always seek to find knowledge, and the same time, we should keep the search for the truth in focus. The advice from that pledge was to aim to be at the top of whatever our chosen profession. As we do so, we would become beacons of hope and light for others; in time, we would know just who we really are as we pursue our "ENDEAVOURS".

The spelling of *endeavour* is correct, that is just the British way of spelling the word! It seems I was destined to live my life in boarding situations, but as I reflect those experiences, they were the ones that allowed me to develop an unbelievable level of independence, strength, and individuality. However, this was so different from the boarding school life. In this place, there were parties (fetes at the Student Union) to attend, trips to take, no one to tell you when to wake up or when to go to bed.

Another change was the meals that were served. Yes, we did have the usual Jamaican dishes of curried chicken, rice and peas, oxtail, steam fish, cabbage and saltfish, but a number of unique dishes from other places in the world crept in. I still cannot find the appetite for "pilau" nor curried lamb. Yes, I loved the curried dishes but lamb. No! It was during those times that many of us became cooking experts of one pot meals. We all secured hot-plates and surprised ourselves with the culinary creations that came from those small units in those small spaces that we called home.

In that new environment of college, you were the captain of your ship. You kept your own schedule, but very often reality would set in and I had to remember that I had to keep a B grade to ensure that I would have the financial support. I worked hard but I enjoyed living.

My first day of classes will never be forgotten. As I entered the lecture room for Introductory Chemistry, there were at least 300 individuals seated in quite anticipation. As I would soon learn, that would not be a constant as we progressed through the program of study. By the time we entered final year, there were fewer women in the upper science classes especially when we began to study Chemistry and Biochemistry. Once again, my father words–"***you can do it***"—helped me as I worked on Organic Chemistry with the addition, substitutions, and redox reactions. Not to mention that in addition to *orals,* there were the *Aural* (one-on-one tests with the professors to verify that you did indeed know the material and was worthy of graduation), to be followed by the final examinations in each upper level course. I graduated with a degree in Chemistry and Biochemistry and that leads to my next life lesson–***You have choices, use them wisely.*** I will explain later! *And remember:* ***You did not need all the material things that you have accumulated in order to live a full and satisfied life.***

Well, enough about those places let me salute those individuals who have impacted my life and provided me with support, encouragement or were just always there for me. This list is important and so I recognize:

Bev G-B (my life-long friend and supporter); Mary H. (my sister); Lilly-June C (my Jamaican support); Yvonne

S (my great friend who know all about my life); Erwin C; Lyubov O (my friend who taught me all things Russian); James H (the headmaster who provided room for me to grow as a science educator); Dianne S-G (my science partner, always!); Norma G (the greatest advisor to my son and daughter, and the best friend anyone could ask for); Greg G (taught me all I needed to know about computers); Dr. Joshua G. (my NY dentist to whom I go even though I live in Georgia); Gil G (my brother-in-law); Talon S. (my traveling partner); Mahasin (my protégé); and Lisa K. (a friend indeed).

Then, the list goes on with Larry W (a genuine friend and the person who never fails to call wherever I am); Valarie A (my younger sister, friend, and supporter); Ari R (a brother who helped me learn about Finland); Cheryl B-J (if you want a secret to be never repeated, tell it to her); Heather C (my confidant, mentee, and supporter); Sergi M (here is my other teacher of all things Russian); Kayla F (a true friend, confidant, and one I respect for her integrity, and strength), Ginger H (the greatest editor whom I have met, she will change your writing, and substitute the best vocabulary in a minute!); Elizabeth C (a guide, mentor, and constant support.

In addition, there is Dr. Bernadette S (the greatest doctor—a doctor to me and my children); and Ruth L (whatever I do and wherever I go, she is my supporter); Keisha S and Miss Annette (the best hairdressers between

New York and Georgia); Winsome J (my niece and constant prayer support); Douglas and Derek G. (my two special nephews); Otis (Rev. Dr. Hugee) my former student and now my spiritual counselor; Jae D (the one who has stood by me during this new change); Madge F (my friend from high school), and Vadis M. (who always calls to see if I am doing well); and all the incredible students that I taught life science, general biology, and Advanced Placement biology. *Make of list of people and places that impact your life, in a positive way, and use them often and carefully. Eliminate the nay-sayers!*

Life Lesson # 11:

You have Choices, use them wisely!

As an educator, you will receive the same respect that you give to students. The process of educating minds involves helping students to construct their own understanding, but above all helping them to find who they are. Teaching is a profession that shapes the minds of our future leaders. As you impact lives, those lives also impact you! The following words were written and presented to me, on a plaque, by one of many students: ***"I owe my success to having listened respectfully to the very best advice and then going away and doing the exact opposite"***[2]. As this young woman delivered the plaque, she explained that she had learned so much from me that she needed to follow my example. She created the words, one for me and one for her! The words always bring me back to reality. I hope wherever she is that she is also using these words as her guide.

As the captain of your ship, you will have to make the

---

2   Laura B.

choices that impact your life, and the lives of others. There was no conscious effort on my part to become a science teacher. I was always interested in science. During my second year at the University of the West Indies, there was a shortage of science teachers in many high schools on the island. Officials from the Department of Education visited the campus and asked those of us who had been given Government scholarships to help during the crisis, on a temporary basis. One other condition was that if we gave 5 years of service, we would not have to pay back any additional student loans. I volunteered and this would be my introduction into educating others. I had hoped to continue my studies as a medical doctor but faith had different plans.

My temporary life as a probationary teacher began at an all-boys school, Kingston College, in the capital of the island. However, in Jamaica, you could only teach for one year at the high school level. At the end of this time, you had to receive the necessary teacher education training to continue in the teaching profession.

I received quick and surprising induction to the process of teaching in the first few days of my sojourn at this school. I was standing on the stage before thirty young men; they were all taller than I was. The Assistant Principal passed by and realized that I was at a disadvantage from the get go since I was not tall enough to see over the podium. Well, he approached me whispered "Do not stand up there; just walk around as you teach! How would I be able to do this?

Teachers always stood at the front and that indicated you were in charge! I couldn't do this! These young men in the 11ᵗʰ grade were only three years younger, but they were giants in my eyes!

Once again my father's words resurfaced–"**You can do it!**"—I gathered the role book and began to go through the attendance. As I called the names— Neil C, Junior F, on to number 38 and ending with Steven V, Collie W. There was a polite response, "Here, Miss". In the meanwhile, the Assistant Principal was helping me behind the scene. He had written my name on the blackboard. In my hour of fear, I had forgotten to even introduce myself to the class, hence the response—Here, Miss. I took the mental stance! I could do this!

The lesson was on the Periodic Table. I had brought all my visuals so I launched right into the teaching process. I never went back to the teacher's podium; instead, I got the students to begin creating their own periodic table by choosing ten elements and finding the symbols, and the use of each element in their daily lives. Remember there were no computers in those days; everyone relied on the required text or a visit to the library for information. Think you could live in that time?

As the young men rose to present their findings, there were snickers, and peculiar sounds coming from their friends, but all too soon, the class ended. The young men filed out row by row, with peculiar smirks on their faces as they said "See you tomorrow, Miss! Tomorrow, what had I taken on? Suddenly, I realized that I was not alone. The Assistant Principal, Mr. D., had stayed with me the entire class! He became my mentor and continued to be my mentor through my early years of teaching. That learning period would continue for the next month. My trepidation gradually subsided as I started on the road to becoming a PRO!

Mr. D explained that this was one of the most difficult groups of students in the grade, but that I would do fine! He never left me for those two weeks. There were lessons learned during those early weeks that have remained with me forever. I believe it is important to share some of those early lessons with others as they enter the teaching profession:

1) *Do not stand at the front of the class, especially if you are my height, 5' 4';*

2) *know your subject matter and be prepared, remember you know more that your students on any given day;*

3) *do not be intimidated by students*—they are just curious children, and 4) *seek help as you need it!*

This was my initiation into the teaching profession. Although I would continue to work at a major bank during my holidays, I had no idea that this would be my calling at the end of my undergraduate training.

"Give instruction to a wise man, and he will be still wiser; teach a just man, and he will increase in learning"[3] *This is mentoring!*

---

3   *Proverbs 9: 9.*

I graduated from the University of the West Indies, in Jamaica W.I, with a Bachelor of Science degree, in Chemistry and Biochemistry.

Graduation From University

Two years later, I began the Master's program in Education and I received the Diploma in Education–Teaching Biology (Distinction). Once I completed the required program of study, I was under the direct supervision of an Education professor from the University for the next two years. At the end of this time, I became a fully trained science teacher. During the next eight years, I was a classroom teacher of General Science, Biology, and Advanced Biology to students in various high schools including an all-boys, an all -girls, and finally a coed institution. In the latter five years, I was a mentor to science teachers.

Life Lesson # 12:

What about those messages you receive from others?
Keep them in a safe place. You will need them
on life's journey to remember that you are a
special individual! There is no one out there
like you. Celebrate your uniqueness!

I have assumed many roles in this life: student, teacher, mother, counselor, mentor, sister, friend, wife, and there may be others that will evolve as I reflect on my life lessons. One role that recurs is that of student. Several of those roles usually intertwined, but the role that is present at every stage is student. I might be called a perpetual learner. I tell myself that I need to be at the top of the game! I read every bit of information that crosses my path; I have grown stronger with an extensive vocabulary. You will see how that gift was used later. Are you on a journey to that place?—focus your life on getting to that place where you envision yourself! Do not be distracted…

I continue to work towards that ideal by using the many notes that have come across my space—from students, colleagues, and friends. Those instruments continued to allow me to maintain my individuality and maintain my strong sense of self:

1) <u>A soul mate</u> – "*Some people believe that there is one "soul-mate"- a soul who has known the other through many lives and seeks the other in each life. I don't believe this, however. I think we have many "soul mates"—mothers, fathers, spouses, friends, and when they "find each other" they begin a journey down a path that they were once familiar with. Each soul mate may only briefly be in this life with the other, but they progress down the path, happier and stronger to re-energize the next life in a more fulfilling encounter. God Bless you for being one of my soul mates.*[4]

2) <u>Student of Advanced Placement Biology</u>, "*Where do I start? This year has been so incredible amazing, and you have been a colossal part of it. From Day One, I knew that I would love AP Bio, and especially its teacher. You made the class come alive, and most importantly, fun to learn. I've learned a <u>lot</u> about biology this year, from mitosis to photons, helicase to reproduction☺, but I've learned how to* **embrace challenges, breathe, extend my potential, be my own person, and especially KMS** *(Keep Mouth Shut). From Bob Marley jam sessions to exam crams to copulating flies to Dolly IMAX to wildebeasts on the Serengeti Plains of Africa to Ms. Frizzle Magic School Bus to Finding Nemo, to the twenty pages for each lab report and there were* **TWELVE** *of them, to daily being*

---

4   Kathy K-G.

amazed by your socks to S's varying accents to T's two-minutes naps to L's constant attempts at entertainment to M's hedgehog presentation to Q's intelligence to K's growth to M's craziness to L's quiet humor to G's genius to J's softness to E's quirkiness to the Box of Toys to that special eating place to Senior Prank Day to my "Things I don't know/ Things I should know list" (it's gotten smaller!) To how much I know I have grown from this amazing class, I thank you! You–literally—have been the best teacher I have ever had simply because you're you and you taught inside and outside the classroom on not just academia but especially this crazy thing, we call life. I thank you so much and cannot wait for you to build your school. This year was incredible. Thank you so much, Love[5]–Laura B.

I have kept albums of all the special messages from students, parents, and colleagues as I journeyed through my teaching experiences. The last time I counted there were ten such books all full with wonderful thoughts and words of appreciation. I go back to them when I need to have my spirit renewed. I encourage you to keep those cards and special thoughts in a place that you can visit in your times of reflection, they are spirit boosters! Also, remember there is something new to learn each day! In the midst of writing this book, my daughter, Trudy, who usually calls everyday phoned in at 10:00 p.m. to tell me the great biologist that there is a special bird—deep blue in color that she saw at

---

5   Laura B.

the zoo. After describing the bird, she explained that it was a Hyacinth.

I could not leave the idea alone. I became wide awake and went to find out more about this new information. This just goes to show that you learn something new every day. Not only am I named after a flower, but a bird is also part of my namesake. This just goes to show that we might never be the same individual to all people. We may be just one individual but we have a wide variety of characteristics which makes us so unique. Focus on your uniqueness; that will set you apart on your journey through life.

As I travel though life, I reflect on those adjectives that were used to describe me and that allowed me to understand how different people have different views of who I am. Some people suggested that I am strong, kind, intelligent, calm, organized, well-spoken, positive, honest, and happy. Other described me as reserved yet outspoken, quiet, and forward. Some have even suggested that I speak the truth with very little thought for the feelings of others (that was what my mother told me). I guess the descriptions depend on the circumstances of my encounters with others. Sometimes, it would appear that we all have split-personalities. I believe that no-one will know you, but you! Therefore, always be true to yourself! You just cannot please and meet the expectations of all the people all the time!

Just be you!

Life lesson # 13:

Find, support, and maintain your moral compass.

My experiences as an educator, and a discussion with my friend and colleague, Kayla F, were the reason for crafting this lesson. As we reflected on our experiences, her question to me was, "When did the change happen in our society to get us to this point where we have developed so much hatred for each other? I did not have an immediate answer, but as I reflected, I explained that it has to do with us, as a people, losing our moral direction—**OUR MORAL COMPASS**—In the time following our conversation, I returned to my experiences in the field of education.

Maybe this is a sweeping statement, but, in my opinion, teaching no longer has the development of children at its core, instead it is the love of **MONEY** and how much one can make! As a result, I have witnessed individuals assuming administrative positions in schools without ever entering a training program. Consequently, people assume that having a degree in Philosophy or Law, without the benefit of a mentorship period, will make one a leader in the school system. The process of getting a job in teaching has become a "cut-throat process" and is now one where people no longer teach children tolerance, love of the environment, and importance of stewardship, integrity, and courage. Instead, the belief exists that anyone can teach!

Educators and leaders are calling for reform, but how will we achieve this when the administrators do not have the necessary skills and training (gained through experience or college training)? Instead, the teaching profession has become a dumping ground for many who have become disillusioned with their present circumstances! We have let loose those individuals on our children. Those educators are in their positions because they knew someone who knew someone. Additionally, many became administrators, by whatever methods, once they failed as classroom teachers

I have seen administrators who do not have the basic skills to evaluate a resume will employ a teacher whose degree indicates Master of Science to teach a science course because they perceive that means the individual is qualified to teach science. At other times, a prospective teacher may state that they can teach a course, and without any investigation, the teacher is employed to teach young minds. In such a case, the teacher is at the same knowledge base as the students or maybe just **one** step ahead. How will children get honest feedback on their questions and thoughts? This level of dishonesty is alive and well and continues unabated in our educational system.

I believe that as the honest, proactive leader empowers teachers to become effective collaborators those teachers will no longer blame each other for failures in student achievement. Instead, teachers will be armed with the techniques that could foster changes within the atmosphere of their classrooms. During that process, teachers, as emerging leaders, will begin to answer the difficult questions that will improve the culture of the school environment. I also believe that when teachers become empowered to create change, they will develop positive self-esteem that flows into the organizational change.

I conclude that if science education in the United States is to improve the focus should be on teacher training and preparation methods. Teachers need support and mentoring. It would be necessary to investigate ways to design and circulate information on teacher development programs geared at improving the level of student academic achievement in science

If the leaders and educators have no idea of how to help children to bring their lives into focus during discussions, students will leave school thinking that the process of learning was meaningless and irrelevant. How will we guide students, when administrators demand that teachers change a student's grade from failing to passing to placate a parent or to give the school a rosy outlook? Before we can enter into reform, administrators must begin to express an ethical compass. This will ensure that teachers will follow their example, and children will learn how to develop integrity and ethics. Without this moral and ethical COMPASS, our educational system is doomed to failure. Several hypothetical questions come to mind! *How could a part-time coach who had no coaching experience become a full-fledge coach; and with no experience becomes a subject teacher; and with no experience takes over management of an educational institution; and with no experience/ training becomes the evaluator of educators? How could an individual with no educational administrative training pertaining become the leader of an educational institution? How can a philosophy degree qualify one to become a science teacher at the highest level? Something is wrong with the picture!!!! It appears that the failures in education result from the loss of our moral compass.* **Word of advice: Look for and find your moral compass. It will be constant force to help you maintain your integrity in your life's journey**

LIFE LESSON #14:

Tough times don't last; tough people do (Ruth L.)

Once I decided I would become an educator, I had to return to do the post-graduate studies in the teaching of biological sciences at the University of the West Indies. I continued to teach for the next ten years, at Kingston College, where I had started my profession as a novice. Then I taught at an all girls' school until May of 1985. For personal reasons, I decided to migrate to the United States.

Well my arrival at JFK airport was another revelation. As I headed to my sister's home, I wondered where the trees and flowers. There was very little space between the houses and many of them looked like the office buildings I had left behind in Jamaica. So, why were the people driving on the right? This was not normal; we drive on the left in Jamaica! There would be so much to learn in the weeks, months, and years to come. Questions flowed non-stop through my mind: What would happen when winter arrive? What really was winter, anyhow? I had only known warm, sunny, or rainy days! Would I be able to make it? Only time would tell!

I arrived in New York City in early May 1985 and I spent the next five months trying to find a teaching position. When I could not find a position, I began to look for any type of job because I had left my children behind in Jamaican and was desperate for them to come to me. Just when I decided that I would give up and return to Jamaica, I got an interview for a teaching position on at Walden High School on July 31st (I had decided that I would return to Jamaica on August 15th).

I had just began my adjustment to the new life, the subways, the buses, the mass of people when Mom passed away—May 13th 1989—the Saturday before Mother's Day. Mom decided that she would never leave Jamaica to reside in the United States even though we begged and pleaded. She believed in her independence and the knowledge that God was able to take care of her. You see, Mom was a praying mother. Often times as a young child, I would walk into a room at home to find her on her knees with her hand raised above her head, eyes closed, and lips moving. The sight was scary at first but as I grew older, I recognized that those were her episodes of praying for all her children. Those observations must have been internalized as I also became and continue to be a praying mother. I will let you know more about that habit, but back to Mom.

We had to find a way to be sure that she was cared for

and had company. Therefore, my sister Madge and I got the helper who had taken care of my children to move in and live with Mom. However, we did ensure that one or the other of her children went home to Jamaica to be with her for as often as we could. At other times, she did agree to visit with us in the United States. On one such visit in January 1989, after four weeks, Mom began to complain that she wanted to go back home. My sister and I tried very hard to get her to agree to stay a bit longer. However, her request to go home became more and more frequent. As a result, we decided that we could not stop her anymore. So Mom got ready to go home, and I never saw her so happy before!

Just before she was ready to leave for the airport, she looked at us and said, "I have just one request, I am going to ask you both to brush up the truth when you tell it to other people". We were both surprised and smiling I said, "Mom, the truth has to be told when it needs to be told. I do not have the time to sweeten it for people". Then she said, "I knew you would say that just like your father, but I had to say that to you!" That would be the last face-to-face conversation I had with Mom because she passed away quietly, the day before I was to take my turn to visit with her in Jamaica, on May 13, 1989.

However, we did honor her other request which was to be sure she was buried in a heliotrope casket. The color heliotrope as I would learn is a shade of purple. Some people might describe it as mauve. Others might explain the color as a mixture of pink and purple. For me as I learned, the name heliotrope has to do with the way the sun moves.

This was no easy feat to find the heliotrope (lavender) colored casket in Jamaica. The task took us five days but I believe through divine intervention, we did in time for the funeral! We buried Mom after a church service and the episode of the "nine-night". By this time, I was a pro at what to expect from the occasion. Mom's service overflowed with her children, grandchildren, nieces, nephews, family, and friends. A perfect example of homecoming for a beloved woman!

I returned home to the United States after the funeral with a feeling of emptiness. I felt as if half of my person was lost. The pain of the loss never goes away; it just becomes easier to bear with time. Maybe it is just my mind but whenever I become discouraged or worried, I find myself surrounded by all things lavender. I find myself wearing purple/ lavender clothes, or the pen I am using to write is purple or the flowers that bloom in the garden are lavender. My cell phone is lavender, my coffee mug is lavender! As I become conscious of the presence of the color, I take comfort in the fact that all will be well. That is the reason, I have surrounded myself with all things of purple/lavender shade and find comfort and love in the color. We all have favorite colors. You too will find your favorite color. Use it to benefit your individuality and life.

I returned to my teaching position at the beginning of

June. The Head of Middle School at Walden High School (later became Walden-Lincoln, later became Trevor Day School) was Evelyn Mc. She was the greatest leader with whom I ever worked. Her guidance and support took me through those years of raising my two children, and kept my focus on the job. I need to say thank you Ev! She taught me how to become organized if I wanted to succeed at being the best mother and educator at the same time.

Life Lesson Extension # 14:

Be organized in every area of your life. That is the key to success! Keep a daily journal in which you prioritize all your daily activities. You should see sticker-pads as one of the most innovative discoveries—Use Them! The wider the range of colors the better!

As I became more organized, I learned to season all the meat that I bought on Saturdays once I came in from the supermarket. I would cook at least two different dinners on Sundays and make small side dishes to accompany our meals during the week. I would do the house cleaning on Saturdays and prepare sandwiches for lunch overnight. I needed to do this because I had to wake at 5:00 am to get everything ready for Trudy, and Gregg who was 3 years old. Trudy grew up very quickly as she helped me by taking good care of herself. She was also very protective of her younger brother. To this day, Trudy continues to be the biggest supporter of her brother. Thank you, Trudy for all your support, but I am so thankful that this training made you into a strong, independent, and wise young woman. Gregg, with your gentle, strong spirit, I know that you and Trudy will always be the biggest supporter of each other!

As I quickly learned, there was no helper in Brooklyn, New York. I had grown accustomed while living in Jamaica to this convenience. I was now on my Own! My first line of duty each week day was to take Gregg to the sitter, Cooper, by 6:00 a.m. every morning. I had to get him ready with all his necessities and then get myself ready for work. Once Gregg was safely with the baby sitter, I would take the *Dollar* cab (Yes, it cost only one dollar for the ride from East 56th Street) to Flatbush/ Junction. I would then take the Number Two train from the Flatbush Station (last/ first stop on the line however, you see it) to West 59th Street in Manhattan. No, that was not the end of the journey! If all went as planned this leg of the journey would take me about 1 hour. Then, I would have to wait for the Number One train! Hopefully, that train would come on time, and if it did, I would spend another 10 minutes on the train. Finally, I would exit at West 86th Street and emerge after five minutes at West 88th Street. I would then have to make the return journey and be back in Brooklyn by 6:00 p.m. to pick up Gregg. Then, I would repeat the cycle again. I did this for seven years! Those were seven years of reflecting and deciding where I wanted to be in life.

It was during those tough times that I met some of the greatest teachers – Susan M. (an outstanding English educator), Ann S (a great artist and teacher), and Ray G (one of the greatest teachers of Social Studies). A few have passed on but I keep them in my memory---Steven E, Cecille L, and Ron. It was also during that time that I learned to grade school work while travelling on the train, and I also passed my time by becoming a skilled needlepoint artist after a period of training from Trudy. Walking also became one of my daily rituals when I could keep my thoughts organized and had the added benefit of maintaining my weight!

When Walden School no longer existed for reasons that were plastered over the news, I faced finding a job that would allow me to support us. Once again, I was searching for a job, but this time I had references and a Search agency for teachers, Manhattan Placement, operated by two of the wisest professionals, Claude and Sylvia K. They have never failed to listen and provide the best employment advice.

So just as I was about to give up again, I got an interview and met with a headmaster, James P. H, who would be my guiding light, support, and powerhouse for many years. In September 1991 and for the next ten years, I was the Head of Science at Brooklyn Friends School, Brooklyn, New York. By the time I ended my journey at the school, I was a veteran science instructor who carried a plethora of experiences to any teaching or administrative position. What I found most rewarding was the ability to teach a wide variety of learners and the freedom to develop new curricular approaches.

During my years of teaching and administrative experiences, I successfully mentored and supervised staff members, coordinated the needs of the science labs, facilitated the needs of promising students (via internships), coordinated science fairs, developed grant-proposals and maintained my active role in continued professional development. In addition, I was also the teacher of 9th grade general biology, 11/ 12th grades advanced and advanced placement biology, and Pre-Engineering elective to juniors and seniors. My children, Trudy and Gregg, would eventually attend and graduate from that institution.

Brooklyn Friends School crafted my path to learning and teaching and I made lasting friendships at that institution. Room 401 was my haven and was always filled with students. In addition, there were many crises, that on reflection, were sources of wonderful memory— 1. The day a student decided to pull on the emergency shower just to see how it worked and flooded the entire area from the fourth floor to the lobby; 2. the day a member of the science department decided to investigate the workings of a laser—BAD IDEA! He almost shocked himself to death; 3. the day a student although being warned not to place any metal objects in the electrical outlets, did so anyway, and sat for several minutes with electricity travelling through his body; 4. the day a student who was told not to eat in the lab, did so anyway and had to be taken to the hospital where his stomach was pumped; 5. the day of our department's holiday party when one staff member decided that he would just stand in the middle of Atlantic Avenue instead of crossing—we did convince him that that was not a good idea and got him safely to the other side!—6. Being lost in my OWN neighborhood of Brooklyn after the party at the Russian Restaurant in Brighton Beach, Brooklyn, New York, and 7. the list goes on and on....

Many of my internalized beliefs have come from those fifteen years of teaching and administrative duties at that Quaker institution in Brooklyn, New York. On a daily basis, I maintained my focus on the tolerance and acceptance of others, and promoted the celebration of cultural, ethnic/racial, gender, and learning differences. I continue to believe that it is my responsibility as an educator to encourage trust and design a safe and comfortable, yet challenging, learning environment for every student that I meet.

I refuse to focus on the negatives during those years, and that is how they will remain. The year before I left Brooklyn Friends School (BFS), I was chosen as Teacher of the Year and was celebrated by the students whom I had taught for fifteen years. Below are some of my favorite students who have impacted my life as an educator at Brooklyn Friends School. Each one made teaching a joy and I know they will go on to conquer the world. In this group, I need to give special attention to Nwanneka C. She has never forgotten my birthday in all those years. She will benefit from the writing of this book. Camille Mc., Myeedah L. and Catherine S will also benefit and I want them to benefit because of their role in helping me to be a better person each day!

Those students taught me the meaning of patience, kindness, how to deal with adversity, laughter, humility, and sharing. Above all, I became the mother to many! After school, my classroom was always filled with students who just wanted to learn because they wanted to learn. School ended at 3:00 p.m., but as Trudy and Gregg grew older, I would find myself spending many late hours and weekend getting my students ready for In-house and External Science Fairs. They just wanted to learn. I include photographs of the students that made a permanent impact on my life, their lives, and our society.

I had the most amusing and amazing teaching experience with the above group of students. Each time I remember one of them, a smile gradually flows over my face. Each individual in those groups was so unique, determined, and just plain smart! Maybe, you can identify me here! I hope that I did impact all the students that I taught; I know for sure that some do remain thankful. In addition, I thank those students who understand the importance to being thankful to those who aided in their successes. I recognize I. V. and B. Sc.

The following excerpt comes from an article by Ife V. *"Her eleventh grade science teacher Hyacinth Foster wound up having a huge hand in Ife's career. "Hyacinth was saying when I was looking at colleges to look into engineering. She said, your mind is geared toward the sciences and not something arts based," and handed Ife a brochure about a Cornell University summer program in architecture for high school juniors. Ife applied and was accepted, and BFS agreed to cover half of the tuition cost. "It was that program that helped seal for me where I wanted to go to college"*[6]

The group of students below gave me all the expertise needed to help them get to college. Through my work with them, I learned about the intricacies of the college admissions process. Thanks, everyone!

---

6   Ife V. in Brooklyn Friends School Newsletter

LIFE LESSON #15:

If everyone likes you then maybe something might be wrong with you.

As a child, I remember how I cried when anyone pointed out one of many faults, and remember we all have faults! It would be many years before I understood what my father was saying through the words—***If everyone likes you then maybe something might be wrong with you***— During my days at boarding school, as I lived with the large number of individuals, I developed my own strong personality. This was a survival technique. Those who failed to find themselves and relied on the affirmations of others would become the followers, and not leaders in life.

Internalize the words of this lesson to keep you always focused on your self-esteem. I find that many people just go around accepting whatever is said to them without developing the art of questioning. You should try not to accept everything you hear. I learned very early in my career that people will have opinions of you that do not mesh with your personal view. Remember, everyone is entitled to his or her opinions of you, but those opinions should never dictate who you are. I knew that the way I came to this conclusion was by finding how I am, liking who I am, and believing in who I am. I always complete what I start and knew there are consequences to every action. ***Check the consequences before you take action. If you are comfortable with the consequences, then go for it.*** If I am willing to accept the consequences then I go full force ahead with my decisions. I quit beating up on me long ago because I know that I am not what others want me to be. I AM ME! Take it or leave it! You cannot please everyone that you meet. ***Learn to love yourself so much that the opinions of others about you will not matter. Remember each individual is entitled to his/her opinion of you.***

LIFE LESSON #16:

When life hands you lemon, make lemon juice add sugar and water to create your own fine drink to quench your thirst.

Those are the unexpected incidences of life when you begin to feel sorry for yourself. However, those are the times when you need to gather strength and begin to turn all the "failures" into the true successes of your life. I have experienced several of those events, but I will address my last teaching position. I always tried to see the good in people so I am going to believe that I could not continue my employment because enrollment declined for that year. Even if my thoughts lead me elsewhere, I am going to stay with the reason because I would then have to focus on the fact that some individuals lack the ability to speak the truth or they have lost their **MORAL COMPASS**.

Whatever was the reason; that gave me the chance to do what I always wanted to do. I refused to focus on the loss of a bi-weekly salary and learned how to become satisfied with living on the minimum. As I think about this time, I have developed a healthy understanding that we need to have very little in order to live a full and satisfied life. In addition, living with little will give each of us a healthy respect when the time of plenty arrives! Since change must come, we just have to have courage and patience.

I considered that it was my time to be at 6:00 p.m. while others were at 12:00 noon, but since this life is a cycle, the wheels will turn and others who were at 12:00 noon will soon find themselves where I am—at 6:00 p.m.! I encourage you to see your 6:00 p.m. as the time to prepare for your eventual arrival at 12:00 noon. I read that the traverses at 6:00 p.m. should be viewed as lessons in the valley of life. Those valley activities will prepare you for your celebrations at the mountaintop. Those thought helped me to remember the words of my favorite song from the Lion King Musical: *The Circle of Life.*

As one of my special birthday treats, one parent sent me front row tickets to the Lion King Musical. That experience remained with me for life. I was in full view of the actors who performed. If I just reached out my hands, I could find myself on the Serengeti Plains with *Simba, Nala, Pumba,* and all the others creatures. For two hours, all my fears and worries evaporated. Finding such a treat is important for our well-being. Each time I need reassurance that all will be well, I listen to the powerful music and become lost in time. Then, I return and refocus!

I mixed my drink. I was not given much sugar, but I

had a great deal of lemon juice. So, I decided to make the best jug of cool drink possible. As a scientist, I decided to measure the ingredients meticulously using the precise proportions to produce the clear-cut results for my drink. I started with what I had, and I researched how to develop skills in online teaching and became a successful online instructor. I thought about the big ideas I needed to work on but never seemed to have the time or opportunity. So, at my son's urging I decided to use the skills and gifts that I had and those that would not require any expenditure—which I did not have! I loved to cook Jamaican and many considered my cooking of oxtail and beans; and curried chicken one of the best!

Hence, a book to include all my favorite Jamaican recipes was born! I completed that assignment with 30 recipes that included special foods, and drinks. Then I moved to develop this book that looked at my life in a positive light, and detailed the lessons that got me to this point. I was careful to measure the amount of lime I would use. In fact, I decided that the lime juice was just for flavor and I could leave out the sour taste and just drink another glass of sugar and water. It tasted just fine! As a result, the negatives in my life were used to empower the positive episodes! I now recognize that the times of our lives involve necessary changes and refer you to one of my favorite books: *Who Moved My Cheese*.[7].

I encourage you to look at some of my other favorite

---

7   Dr. Steven Johnson

books and as you read, you will understand why they remain my favorites. Make a list of your favorite books and go back to them for renewing of your spirit.

1. *Bridge to Terabithia* [8]
2. *Charlotte's Web* [9]
3. *Girl in Hyacinth Blue* [10]
4. *Abel's Island* [11]
5. *Anansi and the Moss Covered Rock* [12]
6. *Rumpelstiltskin* [13]
7. *Great Expectations* [14]
8. *All books by Patricia Cornwell, my favorite writer ever!*

---

8   Katherine Paterson

9   E. B. White

10   Susan Vreeland

11   William Steig

12   Eric A. Kimmel

13   Paul O. Zelinsky

14   Charles Dickens.

LIFE LESSON #17:

If you believe that you are so smart, remember someone else is smarter than you are!

That statement continues to be the reason I continue to be a learner for life. It is important to keep learning and be sure to gain at least one bit of new information each day. ***Remember we all have individual and unique gifts!*** I can cook and explain the intricacies of how to teach. My daughter, Trudy, is gifted at thinking carefully through all business situations, and providing the correct answers to all of the intricate processes. My son, Gregg, has an exceptional gift in his ability to fix anything electrical coupled with the unique understanding of technology. With his critical thinking skills, he is able to solve any problem no matter how difficult it may seem to others.

Some people have the ability to be dance, others can sing, others are good at putting people at ease, some are great painters while others can preach. You have to realize that you were not given all those skills for no reason, so your job is to seek those who have the skills that will help you to solve your problems. As we investigate our skills, we must come to the point where we recognize that we cannot do it all. Someone is going to be more "intelligent" in a specific area than you are. Get help, and help others without letting them feel that they do not know as much you do.

I always keep my favorite memory gem from elementary school in focus and encourage you to commit this to memory. I am not sure of the author but I will quote any way.

"Labor for learning before you grow old, for learning is better than silver and gold. Silver and gold will vanish away, but a good education will never decay!" (Anonymous-Elementary School, Jamaica)

LIFE LESSON # 18A:

Do not be ruled by your ego. It will destroy you!
and
Life's Lesson #18B: Pick your battles and choose
the ones that will help you win the war.

Ego is defined as "the self especially as contrasted with another self or the world"[15]. You must take charge and control this pride which causes you to believe that you are going to fail or that failure is eminent. When your thoughts are overpowered by the imagined negative ideas, you build up this barrier of fear and in order to survive you begin to put everyone down. In my continual readings, I found the best explanation and advice regarding ego has to do with each individual needing to be never wrong. This causes people to find any way possible to defend their ideas, even at the cost of hurting others.

It is the ego that wants us to be always right. I believe that we get into arguments when we believe that we must

---

15 Merriam-Webster's collegiate dictionary; (1999). Springfield, MA:

be right and prove the other person wrong. Decide whether the discussion will enhance your knowledge base or is even necessary; let others believe what they want to believe. Then, decide if you can live with the other person's opinions, in fact does the opinion really matter. If not let it go! It is not that serious. You will find that your life become so simple and you only have to live with you! ***The stimulus will come and as science states you must respond. That response bring about your personal development*** (My science again!) **Do not stay still; keep moving towards your goals!**

Life Lesson # 19:

Light a candle: You may need to see your way in the dark.

Y ou will never come to my home or work without finding a candle burning. I burn a candle to surround myself with light. As a reflected, I believe my early fascinations with candles came from the childhood days when there was no electricity in my home. Our only source of light during those early days was the *Home Sweet Home* lamps, the one we now carefully store away for emergencies in case of a power failure.

The lamps were made of heavy transparent glass, but in later years; they would be made of glass in shades of green, pink, or even red. Each lamp had a receptacle for the oil supply into which the wick extended. The closure had four clamps that would hold the shade in place. The greatest job as a child was to be given the task of cleaning the shade. This was a delicate job where you had to sit still, keep the shade in your lap, and use the softened newspaper to thoroughly clean the shade. You would not be allowed to get up until you were relieved of the shade!

However, cleaning and attending to the lamp was not the real source of my candle lighting fascination! I think the idea came from the times when candles were placed on the Christmas trees because there was no electrical source in those days. I remember how I would wait patiently for those candles to be lit, and although I did not know the danger that could be involved; the candlelight kept me spellbound for those few hours each night. I try not to think about the night when the entire tree was engulfed in flames when no one watched the candles as they burned low! However, that was the source of the lessons I carried with me—NEVER LEAVE A BURNING CANDLE UNATTENDED and ALWAYS SURROUND THE LIGHTED CANDLE IN A CONTAINER OF WATER!

In later years, my own home would have one area devoted to candles and candlesticks in all shapes and sizes. Candles have become a part of my lifestyle and the functions are varied. I use them as I pray each morning and to provide light on my daily path. In one particular place where I worked, I used the candle to surround myself with just one odor because of the constant unpleasant odor emitted from the building. Remember, ***You can only stumble and fall in the dark!***

LIFE LESSON # 20:

I let God's love guide, direct, and inspire me (Daily Word) and finally: You are not paid to worry!

As I travel through life, I developed one constant and that is my daily praying. I have used several sources to help me focus my thoughts but the following books have been my constant companion: *The Daily Word* by Unity. I then connect with *Our Daily Bread* and read the day's passage from the Bible followed by the daily reading. I recall a few passages as I pray for my children, friends, and myself. Finally, I release all my concerns by reading, *Creative Thoughts*

In conclusion, these are the verses that I have live by for as long as I can remember

1. *The Victor by:* C. W. Longenecker.
2. My favourite poem: *If...*Rudyard Kipling.
3. Accept that some days you're the pigeon, and some days you're the statue—Author Unknown.
4. If you are crying over someone, it means you love them

more than you love yourself. There is no sense in such actions!

5. I think people do not understand the real value of having a brother or sister (biological or otherwise)… that is family… always there no matter what.

At this stage of my life, I do not have my usual full-time employment even though I am at the top of my professional capabilities. However, I do not see this as a negative but with each day that passes; I have come to understand that sometimes disappointments are meant to be new doors opening, new opportunities, and a new pathway of life. I learn to **focus, breathe**, and **center myself** each morning knowing that I see myself as the giant standing above those circumstances. I have forgiven all who have offended me long ago so I am at peace with me. That should be your aim in life **AND…**

I live the teachings of my cherished plaque HYACINTH *(from the Greek root name) Hyacinth Flower*

Expression- an individual who is very forward.

Personality – she is mild mannered

Natural – has classic strength and beauty

Emotional – she likes romance

Character – she is an intuitive and honest lady

Physical- is bright-eyed and able

Mental – admired for her wit and cleverness

Motivation – does today what should be done tomorrow (Crystal Skelley, 95).

Epilogue

Your life flows on like a river. Where you are as a person today is a culmination of the fears, worries, triumphs, and happiness. Without those lessons, you would not be who you are, a unique creation of God on a journey to be the best you can be. Keep your stream flowing and stop as often as you can and BREATHE!!!

Remember to MIND YOUR OWN BUSINESS
AND WORK WITH YOUR HANDS!!!

Keep in mind that whatever you need to do, do not delay… Face the challenge and just do it. Do not set limits on what you can do. Whatever you believe, YOU CAN DO IT! As the famous saying goes—"Procrastination is the thief of time." My life continues, my lessons continue, may your lives be ones of continual successful learning!